Avalanches

BY PATRICK MERRICK

Published by The Child's World®
1980 Lookout Drive • Mankato, MN 56003-1705
800-599-READ • www.childsworld.com

ACKNOWLEDGMENTS
The Child's World®: Mary Berendes, Publishing Director
Olivia Gregory: Editing

PHOTO CREDITS
© bikeriderlondon/Shutterstock.com: 18; Deepfrog17/
Dreamstime.com: 17; Dmitry Naumov/Shutterstock.com: 15;
eugvas/BigStock.com: cover, 1; franky242/BigStock.com:
13; Kapu/Dreamstime.com: 10; Mikadun/Shutterstock.com:
5; Mikhail Pogosov/Shutterstock.com: 9; Scattoselvaggio/
Dreamstime.com: 7; Strahil Dimitrov/Shutterstock.com: 21

ISBN 9781631437625
LCCN 2014945413

Printed in the United States of America
Mankato, MN
November, 2014
PA02245

ABOUT THE AUTHOR

Patrick Merrick was born in California and spent much of his early life moving from town to town and from state to state. Patrick now lives in Minnesota with his wife and children. When not busy teaching school, writing, or parenting, Patrick enjoys the occasional nap.

Table of Contents

Avalanche!

Avalanches
are also called
"snowslides."

Worldwide,
avalanches
kill about 150
people each year.

High in the mountains, clouds cover the sky. The steep slopes are covered in deep snow, and soon more begins to fall. All of the countryside is quiet and calm—but there is danger.

Suddenly, a large amount of snow breaks loose from the mountain. A white wall of snow and ice rumbles down the slope. Everything in its path is buried. An avalanche is born!

An avalanche tumbles down the slopes of France's Mont Blanc. The tallest mountain in the Alps, it stands 15,781 feet (4,810 m) high.

Mountains and Snow

Areas with very steep slopes are especially prone to avalanches.

Snowy drifts that hang over cliffs are common areas for avalanches to start.

Avalanches can happen anywhere there are mountains or steep hills. In the United States, the Rocky Mountains have most of the avalanches. Other countries that have a lot of avalanches are Peru, Canada, China, Austria, and Switzerland. And one area in France has over 500 avalanches every year!

A snow cornice is an overhanging edge of snow on the ridge of a mountain. Here you can see cornices at the top of this mountain. As the overhanging areas become heavier with snow, they can break loose—starting an avalanche.

Avalanche Beginnings

The best time for an avalanche to occur is 24 hours after a snowfall of over 12 inches (30 cm).

Skiers, snowboarders, and mountain climbers often cause avalanches.

It is hard to imagine how snow can be dangerous. To understand how avalanches work, you must learn about the snow itself. Snow is made up of tiny crystals. As the snow falls throughout the winter, the crystals pile on top of one another like the layers of a sandwich. With each snowstorm the layers keep growing and growing. In the mountains, some snow piles can be as much as 40 feet (12 m) thick!

With all that snow sitting on the side of a steep mountain, the layers can slide over one another and come tumbling down the mountain. This is an avalanche! To start the snow layers sliding, all it takes is a **vibration**, or small movement. Even sounds such as the voices of people or faraway trains can start an avalanche.

This huge avalanche is rumbling down Donguzorun, a mountain in Russia. It is 14,613 feet (4,454 m) high.

Different Types

Since there are different types of snow, there are different types of avalanches. One type of avalanche is called a **dry snow avalanche**. In a dry snow avalanche, the snow is like fine powder. As one snow crystal hits another, they start sliding down the hill. Soon the whole mountain of powder comes rumbling down. A dry snow avalanche can reach speeds of 200 miles (322 km) per hour!

Another type of avalanche is called a **slab avalanche**. In this type, the snow is packed very tightly. With the smallest vibration, huge chunks of snow begin sliding down the mountain. On February 5, 1983, a chunk of snow that was 30 feet (9 m) thick started an avalanche in Alaska. When the avalanche was over, the valley below the mountain had enough snow in it to fill 22 football fields.

Smaller dry snow avalanches are called "sluffs."

Slab avalanches move at about 80 miles (129 km) per hour.

Slab avalanches are the deadliest type of avalanche.

Here you can see a dry snow avalanche as it roars down some mountains in the country of Georgia.

Lots of Damage

Avalanches can block roads for days until people can clear away the snow.

Power lines can easily be snapped by an avalanche, causing entire towns to lose power.

When snow from an avalanche melts, it can cause flooding in certain areas.

Avalanches can do a lot of damage. The power of an avalanche can destroy a whole town. The wind made by an avalanche can also be dangerous. The falling snow pushes the air in front of the avalanche at very high speeds. In 1962 an avalanche in Switzerland produced winds that snapped trees in half.

The effects of an avalanche can be seen for a long time after the snow stops moving. That's because an avalanche changes the land around it. Avalanches carry huge amounts of dirt from one area to another. One avalanche can move as much dirt as a river will move in one year.

You can see the damage this avalanche caused in Austria.

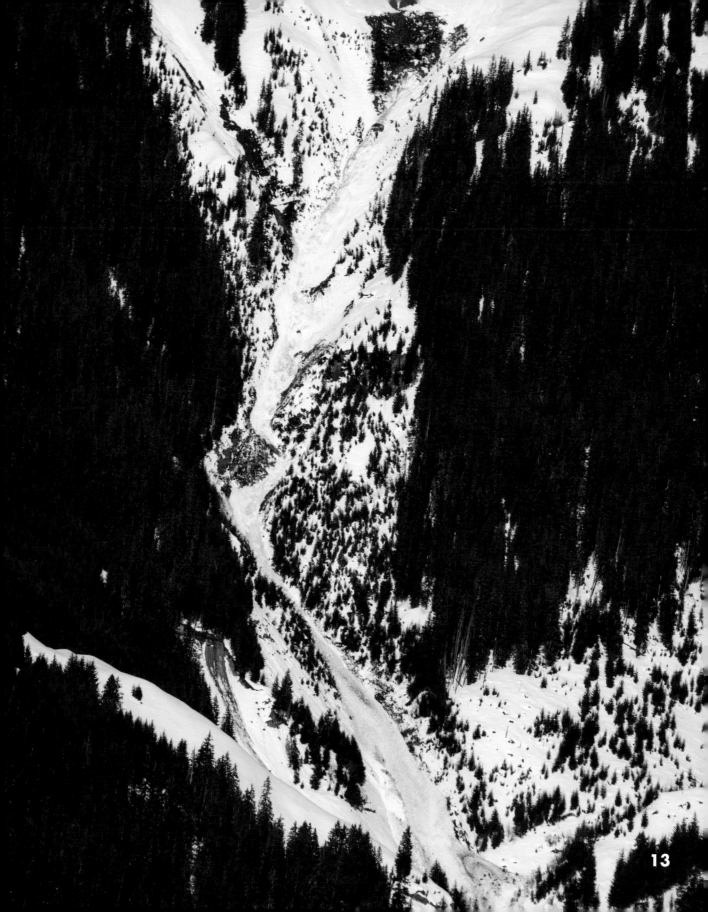

Stopping Avalanches

People in some areas use nets made from strong steel cables to lessen avalanche damage.

Some towns build deep dams or mounds of earth to steer avalanches away from areas where they could cause damage.

Avalanches are a part of nature. There is no way to stop them from happening. However, people have learned ways to slow down the moving snow. Many people build fences or walls on the sides of mountains. People also plant trees as a natural wall to stop the snow. In some areas, people even make paths for the snow to follow. These paths lead the snow away from roads and towns.

In some mountain areas, people have built **snowsheds** to lead the snow away from the roads. A snowshed looks like a slanted roof over the road. When an avalanche hits the snowshed, the snow flies through the air and lands on the other side of the road.

The top of this snowshed in Taiwan is slanted so the snow will fly away from the road.

In some parts of the world, military troops are in charge of controlling avalanches.

Many ski areas have avalanche control teams. They start avalanches on purpose to clear dangerous areas. This keeps skiers and snowboarders safe.

Some scientists start avalanches on purpose. By starting smaller avalanches, scientists can clear away the heavy snow before a larger avalanche has a chance to start.

To start a controlled avalanche, scientists find a patch of heavy snow that is hanging over the edge of a steep cliff. Then they clear all the roads and surrounding areas of people. Finally, they use a large cannon to send explosives into the snow. The blast shakes the snow and starts a small avalanche.

Here you can see a ski patrol member tossing explosives to start an avalanche.

Staying Safe

If you spend time in the mountains, it is important to be prepared. Before going hiking or skiing, make sure that you have the right equipment. When you are traveling on mountain slopes, always stay with a group. Most important, never go into unmarked or dangerous areas. Avalanches can happen without warning, so it is very important to stay in safe areas.

The biggest problem from being trapped in an avalanche is lack of oxygen.

If you're caught in an avalanche, try to clear a space near your face to breathe.

After two hours of being trapped in avalanche snow, very few people survive.

This sign warns U.S. skiers and hikers to stay out of an area.

The word "avalanche" has been used since 1744.

Cracking and "whooping" noises can often be heard just before an avalanche occurs.

So the next time you are in a snowy, mountainous area, look around. Can you see any drift of snow hanging over a cliff? Are there any signs warning people to stay out of certain places? Make sure to follow directions and stay safe. If you do, then you can enjoy the snowy outdoors without worrying about an avalanche.

This huge snow drift on a mountaintop is sure to cause an avalanche.

Glossary

dry snow avalanche (DRY SNOW AV-uh-lanch)
Dry snow avalanches happen when fine, powdery snow falls down a mountain.

slab avalanche (SLAB AV-uh-lanch)
Slab avalanches happen when huge chunks of snow fall down a mountain.

snowshed (SNOH-shed)
A snowshed is a roof that is built over a mountain road. When an avalanche hits a snowshed, the snow is sent flying to the other side of the road.

vibration (vy-BRAY-shun)
A vibration is a very small movement. Even a small vibration can cause an avalanche.

To Find Out More

In the Library

Bishop, Amanda, and Vanessa Walker. *Avalanche and Landslide Alert!* New York: Crabtree, 2005.

Duden, Jane. *Avalanche! The Deadly Slide.* Logan, IA: Perfection Learning, 2000.

Shone, Rob. *Avalanches & Landslides.* New York: Rosen Central, 2007.

Walker, Jane. *Avalanches and Landslides.* New York: Gloucester Press, 1992.

On the Web

Visit our Web site for links about avalanches:

www.childsworld.com/links

Note to Parents, Teachers, and Librarians: We routinely check our Web links to make sure they're safe, active sites—so encourage your readers to check them out!

Index